THE COVID-19
&
THE COMMANDER IN CHIEF

SURVIVAL MANUAL

RICARDO NUNDI

War Correspondent

EMMI PUBLICATIONS

Copyright © 2023 by EMMI Publications
All rights reserved. No part of this publication may be reproduced, distributed or transmitted in any form or by any means, without prior written permission of

EMMI PUBLICATIONS
Edgewater, NJ 07020

Publisher's Note: This book is based on true events. It reflects the authors present recollections of experiences over time.

Author - Ricardo Nundi - (Nundi Your Business)
Copy Editor — Claudia Mason
Cover Design — EMMI

ISBN -979-8-218-38704-4

Disclaimer: The author has no political affiliation. These thoughts are just observations and never judgment. The Publisher and the author assume no responsibility for errors, inaccuracies, omissions, or any other inconsistencies herein and hereby disclaim any liability to any party for any loss, damage, or disruption caused by errors or omissions.

In Memory Of

Mrs. Clara Richards, Mrs. Carolyn Lockard, Mrs. Bobbie Jordan,
Mr. Chet Johnson, Mr. Steve Issacs, Mrs. Ena B. Nunes,
Ms. Demi Argiropoulos, and Bishop William P. DeVeaux

A Special Thank You to,

Mrs. Irma W. Hawkins
Mrs. Barbara Holman Reynolds Robinson

Quote ; "Handle Hard Better" - Kara Lawson

Summer 2022

i· RICARDO NUNDI

Table of Topics

The Beginning:

Why is it even called Covid 19 and ....

Covid 19:

The Vladivostok Candidate:

The Getting Dressed Part:

Now you JERK me down to sleep:

Feeding Yourself during ....

 A Funny Story ......

Can you say Leadership?

03 May 2020 Death tolls:

The curious case of the missing face masks?

The Original 13 Colonies and Covid 19:

The Antifa Swindle:

The Photo Opportunity:

Cont...

The stimulus Check Blues:

Is it me or what? 02 July 20:

July 02, 2020 : Covid 19 numbers:

Instead of M.A.G.A it should really ...

He knew that Covid 19 was dangerous...

Sept 18, 2020:

The Election Drama:

As of July 2022:

What else? The Supreme Court!

Epilogue (Ep.I.loge)

Commander in Chief Number 45:

Surviving the Commander in Chief and the Covid-19 Wars

Vision: Surviving the Endgame Strategy: Educate the Ignorant at ALL Times

Vision Statement: Your self-defense is truly your only defense.

Action Plan: Stay ALIVE by Any and ALL Means Necessary

Commander in Chief: a noun. A head of state or officer in supreme command of a country's armed forces or an officer in charge of a major subdivision of a country's armed forces, or of its forces in a particular area. In the United States, as of 19 April 2020, the Commander in Chief is President Donald J. Trump. The Secretary of Defense is Mark Esper. Chairman of the Joint Chiefs of Staff is Mark A. Milley. The military budget is 718 billion (2018) and there are 700,000 civilian and 2.8 million military employees. Note: the 45th President of the United States last name is spelled

Trump here in the USA, but in Germany it really was and is spelled Trumpf, so this is how you will see it spelled.

Covid 19:

COVID-19- CO stands for corona. VI stands for virus. D stands for diseases. Also known as 2019 Novel Corona Virus or 2019-nCoV. Covid 19 is a new kind of Corona Virus. Like MERS-CoV or SARS-CoV or SARS-CoV-2 (which is a beta coronavirus), they all seem to commonly cause upper respiratory tract illnesses. Corona viruses are a large family of viruses that are common in people and some animal species. They originally start with animals and then infect people, and then spread between people. There were 18 Covid's before this strain. What does it do to be so deadly?

War: / wor/ noun. Plural noun: Wars. A state of armed conflict between different nations or states or different groups within a nation or state. Survival: /ser vivel/ noun. The state or fact of continuing to live or exist, typically despite an accident, ordeal, or difficult circumstances.

Surviving: / ser- viv-ING/ adjective: Remaining alive, especially after the death of another or others. Continuing to exist. Remaining intact.

My observations: History will judge us all on how we handled this precarious time in human history on this planet which is the 3rd planet from the sun in this, our galaxy. It will also judge us how we did or did not do the right thing regarding the preservation of human life and preserving the world for all future generations. It will judge us because of what we were afraid to do, or say or act, and really on how we handled ourselves during such a trying and complex time in our country and for the entire world. It will judge us on what we could or should have done better. Was everything worth the hard decisions and choices that most certainly were made for the betterment of all of us? Because our fearless leader President #45 was a businessman not a politician nor an academic, and all that he knows is that the object of any business, plain and simple, is to make money, and for any corporation the object is to make money for the shareholders. So, he was committed to only do what he thinks that he knows and nothing else, and nothing will ever change this fact of life in his mind. He does not care about anyone or anything outside of his own sphere of influence and thus he only cares about his history and no one else'. If this was France, and #45 was its fearless leader, the French people would have already rioted hard core in the streets, because after all, the French are who we modeled our whole political system and the concept of the word Democracy. Because France, our savior during the early years of our country, gave us aid and brought leadership against the King of England and his crown taxes.

The Beginning:
Around Thanksgiving 2019 or very soon after it, I started to see Asian people on the metro rail trains or just about everywhere wearing masks. Curious I thought, because Asian cultures tend to be very polite and trained to follow rules, and so anytime most Asian people are sick, they wear the masks so that they will not spread their sickness to others, but strangely this was something else. I knew that Asia, especially China was dealing with some kind of new flu or something, but the US news media and other outlets were focusing solely on the

antics of **President #45's** impeachment process, and really nothing else. Sure, they were reporting about it, but not in any informative sort of way, shape or form, like it really was not a true newsworthy story here in the **US of America**.

December 2019 arrived and about 2 weeks before Christmas, things seemed amiss, but on the surface, things still seemed to be normal, and no one in any kind of leadership position seemed alarmed or upset. Was there anything really wrong? But things in China were drastic and getting tighter, as evidenced by the air bombing and water blasting of all Chinese cities with bleach and cleaning supplies. So, what was really going on?

January 2020 and all hell (excuse my French) began to break out **ALL** over the planet, and still the US of America's leadership was acting like this virus called the Corona virus was no big thing. Why was the US of America President # 45 acting like it did not affect him? He basically sat on his hands for 3 weeks before he did **ANYTHING**! His wait and see approach, which really means that anytime you are in a wait and see mode about anything; then you are just basically **MAKING** things up as you go along with no real plan. But in this case was that truly the plan all along? Was this part his endgame strategy all along that him and his National Socialist Posse members had devised to assume worldwide control so all this back and forth and lack of real information appeared to be working in their favor?

Who are these people you are thinking? Well, these are the people that lost World War 2, the Axis powers: Germany, Italy, Japan, South Africa, Spain, etc. So once **WW2** was over, they spread about all over the world, and just bided their time, letting others do their evil bidding until the time was truly right. So, in 2020 look at the countries where people with this mentality have assumed leadership or really **CONTROL** over key countries, (USA, UK, Hungry, Brazil, Australia, etc.). Do you realize that they **ALL** are using the very same strategy: stoking racial fears, suppression of the news in all its various forms, misinformation, mis direction of information, destruction of nature, using immigration to build walls and create isolation?

Because of their hatred of diversity in all its many forms and shapes, they want to change the courts and the laws in their favor. But enough of that, which is a totally different back story that happens to intertwine with the Covid -19 outbreak. So back to the ranch, with conflicting information out there many people have been dupped into believing that this Covid-19 is not really that serious or in reality does not affect them. Why didn't #45 spring into action when the first reports were official that Covid-19 was in the lower 48 states in January 2020? Why did he fire all the main people at the CDC, the year before all of this, who could have begun the process to make a real difference? Maybe he wanted it to get worse so that he could then become a **WAR**-time President or **WAR**-time Commander in Chief. Here in the US of America, no sitting President has ever not been re-elected in any time of war. That is why #45 had been trying to create something that he could then use to stay in office or use so that people would not vote him out of office when voting time arrived.

Remember that he is just a tool for his national socialist posse, and always remember that he is a businessman and not a politician, so he has always marched to a different beat of the drummer. He had no intentions of saving other people. He only represents or shows leadership skills to a very small percentage of the people who needed him in office so that they could remain in the business of the business of stealing money. He has never ever represented **ALL** Americans, no matter what he says or tweets, or spews out of his mouth. Remember that he is the very same person, who hired Black people to go to his campaign rallies, so that they could get beaten up by denouncing his Make America Great Again campaign. They emotionally spiced up the crowds and created excitement for some racists with some good old-fashioned race baiting grandstanding. So, whenever he talks about anything just realize that he will then turn around, in twenty minutes or less than that, on numerous occasions, and say something totally opposite that totally contradicted everything that he just had said was his truth. He wanted Americans to be safe, yet as the stock market crashed and he also lost money, he then wanted folks to go back to work. He said it was safe, and the churches would be filled by Easter. When clearly, he nor any of his family never ever were seen attending any church function from his Day 1 in office. This Covid 19 required most Asian nations to shelter in place anywhere from 8 to 14 weeks, which is not 14 days or 2 weeks.

I would have felt more comfortable about this whole thing if the information that we were receiving was reliable and on point and on time. Example: # 45 had been having daily news conferences on Covid-19, with some of the most tired and haggard looking folks imaginable. Not one person on the podium said anything assuring and comforting as regards information. Example: Testing. Why not use the WHO (World Health

Organization) test kit, (because they wanted to wait to create their own test or stall with the information as more citizens died for no reason)? Why not look at places like Germany who has low numbers of affected citizens and see what they are doing to combat the virus (they are testing scores of people each day with a reliable test which is detecting sick people.)? Why were we not seeking information from Cuba and China and Asian, and worldwide med-ical communities thus getting proven and reliable methodologies to battle this man-made virus. Why did it seem that any reporter in the briefing who asked real and great questions was shunned and ostracized? And why were the reporters who got to answer questions all handpicked it seemed to ask questions that really did not matter or were used to spread mis information to the ignorant or lowly educated citizens in our great society?

This whole Covid 19 was so surreal because it was like we the citizens of the great society or experiment must use our own self wits and/or resources, to come up with a cure or method to combat this virus on our own. We were alone in our struggle to defend ourselves, and the President #45 acted like he did such a great and wonderful job considering that he realistically had to have known about this since December for sure. Covid-19 is a biological weapon that threatens ALL sovereign nations national security interests. The NSA National Security Agency had to know about this! That is, its job to protect all U.S. of A's security interests.

Now all the information that is swirling all over the internet may or may not be true, but our countries leadership and command structure did not even debunk if it is true or not true. Example: there were a growing number of reports that were coming from the worldwide medical community that Ibuprofen or Advil is not to be taken because of a growing fear that the virus replicates by the 10 or 100 times when it encounters it. Or that zinc or vitamin C or honey or the Elderberry syrup all are effective against the virus because they all tend to build up your immune system and thus by any means necessary should be taken or used daily. Or that the virus is airborne and can live in the air for up to 3 hours and up to 9 days on metals and plastics. Or that this virus is passed from person to person within 3 feet or less, and that with this being the hay fever time of the year, anyone who is infected who sneezes and or spits is releasing the virus into the air, where it can live for up to 3 hours. Or that the virus cannot live in UVA rays, which is sunlight, so it is vitally important to always stay in sunlight if possible. Or it is important to always cover your head and hair because it can get on your clothes and in your hair or beard, and it can even be on the bottom of your shoes or sneakers that you then track into your house and all over your living space. The Chinese medical authorities have highly suggested that you leave you shoes at your front door and that you shower at least two or three times daily and that you even more importantly either shower or bath anytime that you come inside from the outside.

Why is it even called Covid 19 and what really happened to Covid 1 through **18**? Is Covid-19 a biological weapon that got loose sideways, and at this point we really could give a damn (excuse my French) who did what to release this plague? Just like the Ebola virus from pandora's box, but what we need is factual and intelligent and timely information that is on point and reliable.

BECAUSE our survival depends upon knowledge, and we must get that knowledge in a faster manner than we ever have had before. My so-called leaders did not get up off their hind parts and act, and thus many more Americans died when it just was not truly necessary. How do you choose who must or will die? On a side note, if I had to vote right at that very moment to get #45 out of there, it would have been for Governor Cuomo from the Empire State, who in my humble observation, has provided much more boots on the ground type of leadership skills and information than either Joe Bidden or Senator Sanders, both had at this very crucial moment in US history.

But I also know that #45 dragged his feet and held back resources to those states that the Governors who were not in agreement with his crack is whack type of policies and his classic make it up as he goes along procedures. The Governors were being held hostage so to speak and a lot of them seemed just go along with #45's BS and so-called gamesmanship that he was playing. The key is that we must **ALL** survive this new age Middle Passage through this modern-day Alice in Wonderland rabbit hole. **WE** must defend ourselves, and pass information to others as soon as we can determine if it is reliable **AND** realistic. My rule on that is, if it comes through anyone in any medical community type of environment, then proceed with caution, but proceed you should. Do not expect any help or aid, from anyone higher than your state and or local levels, which means that the Federal Level was non-existent. **Always remember that dumbness can be hereditary, but stupidity is a choice!** Please make wise choices that will ensure that you stay alive at all costs by any means necessary. Example: just because Lester Holt does not say this or that, then it is not true? I am not singling him out, because I trust him on some intrinsic level that I think is related to culture. For me, he is the current kind of Obama news figure of the original 3 main television news stations (CBS, ABC, and NBC). That is not a great decision my fellow citizens, because you should be able to make up your mind and use your own methods of reasoning to come up with your own conclusions and or decisions. Always educate the ignorant.

Covid 19: hum 18 Covids Before This Strain, and What Does It Do to be So Deadly?

The real question is why does this virus create havoc in some places and yet barely touch others? There just seems to be no real answers as to why it effects one place, and not really affects others. Some folks suggested hot climates, were spared, but in places like Brazil, and Indonesia and the Dominican Republic that was not the case. But one curious statistic was that countries with relatively younger populations did not experience the full-blown turn on the news every day and see how many people have died in your country syndrome. So, for example in Africa, which is the world's youngest populations, there were only about 45,000 reported cases early on, from a total population of 1.3 billion people from 54 countries, with more than 60 percent of the 1.3 billion under age 25. But this was not always the norm either because in other places with older populations, for example Japan, who has the world's oldest population, about 130 million, there had only been about 520 recorded deaths. *So, what is the real deal Holyfield? (*statistics were current at the time of this writing)

The Vladivostok Candidate:

There is a great movie, in 1962 that starred the one and the only Mr. Frank Sinatra along with both Sir Lawrence Harvey and Ms. Janet Leigh that was called the Manchurian Candidate. It was re-booted, in 2004 for a younger audience, as Hollywood tends to always do, starring the great Mr. Denzel Washington and Mr. Liev Schreiber, and both were films about how they (China in the first film and Arab/Eastern looking foreign Multinational corporation, the Manchurian Corporation in the re-booted version) brainwashed USA soldiers to perform acts against the United States of America's political structure and government to do their evil bidding. The original film, about Cold War sleeper agents, is considered a classic here in the USA, and I enjoy watching it anytime it is being shown. Sir Lawrence Harvey was the poor brainwashed individual (you can substitute the word fool) who was under the control of his evil and sinister Chinese overlords until the very end of the movie. It also was stunning to see how the whole movie was written and acted out, because it seemed totally believable and real. The film showed how a person might be converted into becoming an unknowing and unfeeling tool of a communist master.

The rebooted version (2004) was about Desert Storm sleeper agents in the future America were Xenophobic, and the defacto Marshall Law. Severe environment degradation and increasing corporate control were the norm, and therefore the need to control people by the national socialist or imperial minded corporations to reach a desired end, was essential and necessary. I enjoyed them both for their twists and turns, but the differences between both films, seem to be the meanings of who were the bad guys, which seemed shadowy and did not seem very clear in the second film. Well, if art imitates life and life imitates art, then what we are experiencing these last 3 years of Mr. Donald Trumpf (which is the real historic Deutschland spelling of his family's name) must be a version of the live Vladivostok Candidate who is doing the evil bidding of his Russian masters, namely one named Mr. Putin. He also just happens to be the ex-KBG high up and a man of mystery officer who after the USSR broke up somehow slipped in there to become the President of Russia and is the one who now controls the stockpile of guided atomic missiles, and weapons arsenal. Now Vladivostok (which means Conqueror of the East) happens to be a city in Russia that is in the most western part of Russia on the Golden Horn Bay peninsula area, and it is the largest Russian port on the Pacific Ocean and the home port of the Russian Pacific Fleet. The city is not far from the Russian borders with China and North Korea. It has always been an extremely important place where all types of commerce and trade occur every day and a place that, if the rumors are true, has become the purported main hub of the Russian underground sex trade.

It has become, according to rumor, the undisputed transfer point of the global underground sex trade ever since Uday Hussain, yes Saddam crazy son, the porno King was taken down in Iraq. Someone had to fill that void that Uday Hussein left when he was killed and just like in the Netflix series Narcos has shown, someone always does.

It appears that this is the very same sex trade highway that Mr. Jeffery Epstein was able to control here in the Americas and became the supplier of a uber sex trade operation for a virtual who's who of rich and powerful men.

But the real Wizard of Oz behind the curtain the whole time has been the savvy, calculating and brilliant Mr. Putin, who first was able to control the KGB (the USSR version of the CIA—C e n t r a l Intelligence Agency), and then the entire country of Russia, and who is the real puppet master. He, being an old KBG leader means that he has the dirt's dirt everyone both legally and illegally rich, and he is the one that has been pulling all the strings the whole damn (excuse my French) time. He has his far-reaching tentacles in every Great 8 (Core) country, and he lets nothing stand in the way of his methods and objectives. For example, he put the richest man in Russia (in 2003 worth 15 billion dollars, and Number 16 on the Forbes worldwide list of billionaires), the Yukos oil tycoon **Mikhail Khodorkovsky**, in jail for some bogus trumped (interesting choice of words, if I do say so myself) up charge that did not even sound right to anyone in the entire world! Then had a whacky trial which conveniently convicted him in 2005 for 9 years. In December of 2010, while he was still in prison serving aout his time; he re-charged him and his business partner of money laundering and embezzlement. By all accounts, **Mr. Khodorkovsky**, was the one in Russia who was doing great and wise things with his money (like Open Russia 2014) to make his much beloved Russian homeland a much better and vibrant place in the world.

The real deal Holyfield intel shows that he was going to run for President of Russia head-to-head against Mr. Putin. By all accounts from boots on the ground in Russia, he had Mr. Putin and his hench-people on the run, and would have won most say, if he had ever been given the chance to go head-to-head at the voting polls with Mr. Putin, the self-described President for Life in Father Russia. But the crazy part in this whole sordid tale of clashing egos running a muck is that Mr. Putin had somehow stolen all or damn (excuse my French) near all of **Mr. Khodorkovsky's** money (he was only left with somewhere between 100 to 250 million when he finally was released or pardoned from prison by none-other that Mr. Putin himself).

Mr. Putin in the shadows of the organized crime syndicate, which was once called the KGB, now somehow in a blink of an eye, like Jeannie of *I Dream of Jeannie* television fame, became one of the richest men in the world. Talk about being a real straight up **OG** (Original Gangster). How does an individual that has exhibited unchecked criminal behavior become in charge of everything like prisons, and the economy and military and nuclear stockpile? This is the same person who has poisoned outspoken dissidents of his, in other countries, and maybe it is just me, but isn't intentionally poisoning someone just because he or she calls you out in public for what you are, called murder just about everywhere else in the world? How about the way that he has influenced Mr. Trumpf (VC) into allowing Russia to become a world class superpower without the slightest hesitation or questions, as if he were under his mind control.

All the previous USA Presidents up until # 45(VC) have always found a way to check Mr. Putin's interests and his personal ideas of manifest destiny and do so in a way that keeps the playing field both level and honest for the betterment of the whole world. None of that Houston Astro's garbage can banging signaling tactics here Mr. Putin! We see you and we hear you and we will stop you, as in check/checkmate. So, what is it that he has on Mr. Trumpf (VC)? Could it be that he knew about Mr. Trumpf's (VC) knowledge of and somehow connections to the sex/slave global pipeline, and he somehow used this information against Mr. Trumpf (VC) to assist Mr. Trumpf (VC) to rig the USA's Presidential election? So that once Mr. Trumpf (VC) became President, he would be powerless to say no to him, and thus make him uncheckable? The sitting USA President turned a blind eye and a deaf ear like any truly brainwashed individual would do.

Mr. Putin has consistently played both sides of the coin, and he is brilliant in his movements and tactics in the overall game plan, just like he was a grandmaster of chess. He wants to bring Russia up into the so called First World (the Core), even though it has always maintained itself as a semi-periphery nation. To do so, all the strong economies of the Core nations must be weakened so that every country will sink down to Russia's level or North Korea's level, thus in a sense leveling the economic playing field in an inverse sort of manner.

Mr. Putin who is a straight up big game hunter type, is the one I feel who could have released the Covid-19 in China in the first place, to get the Chinese to think that it was the USA who was responsible for the release in their country in Wuhan that houses China's infectious diseases center. Covid – 19 was then released around the entire world and especially here in the USA to help Mr. Trumpf (VC) to be able to enact the 1950 War Powers Act, which suspends Miranda and the rite of Habeas Corpus, creating a military state. Here in the USA Mr. Trumpf (VC) led the battle of Covid 19 as seen by some as a war. Then Mr. Trumpf (VC) could naturally get re-elected by the blind and terrorized USA population.

This is the real reason why Mr. Trumpf (VC) effectively played dumb about Covid-19 attacking Far East Asia since late 2019, and sat on his hands for roughly 3 months, in early 2020 before he even felt compelled to act here in the U.S. because he needed the time to let the respiratory virus spread and do its dirty work worldwide. Then the national socialists will really be able to link up because each country will have mobilized their armies to protect their homelands from the Covid-19 enemy, and military law and justice will rule the day. This is the same blueprint that Mr. Hitler first described and then used to perfection in his brilliant but decidedly evil self-help book called *"Mein Kampf"*. (Do you notice that both Kampf and Trumpf (VC) both end in mpf?) Is this then the national socialist endgame, and Mr. Putin is and has always wanted to be a dictator or some type of imperious rex type of individual.

Look at places like North Korea, Russia, Italy, Philippines, Brazil, Syria, Israel, Saudis Arabia, Malaysia or Hungry, or some say Australia. Any country for that matter that has a despot at the helm, and in control of steering their nation's ship in the right direction can easily turn in another direction. If you can use logical thinking and connect the dots, you will see the same pattern of behavior in all these countries. They suppress the news, weaken and destroy the infrastructures, promote and disseminate mis information (think of the fake news quotes), oppress the lower rungs of society's ladder, create and then stir up nationalistic feelings regarding Immigrants, exhibit isolationistic behaviors with talks of building walls and/or fences and racial tendencies, steal and rob the national treasurers of the people all in the name of these very same people! They pick right up where Mr. Hitler and his cronies left off at the end of 1945 because they were stopped cold in their tracks by the U.S. of A's heroic middle class. So, to be able to execute this well thought out and devised operation whose code name is Endgame, the USA must be brought down to its knees and if it crumbles, then the world crumbles, because the USA effectively has been protecting the world's nations and its populations since FDR's sovereign reign.

Mr. Trumpf (VC) is the lackey or tool, as in fool, the same type of poor fool in the movie the Manchurian candidate, that was played by Sir Lawrence Harvey, who could not even help himself, to do the right thing even if he wanted to. After all he is not a politician, he is a money grubbing and loving businessman.

As a businessman, he most importantly knows all the dirty and semi-illegal tricks that turn a buck. Somehow after a conversation with Mr. Putin, (that he always tends to have with his fellow would be dictators and con artists), the USA has somehow purchased N-95 Covid-19 masks from the Russian Government, when Russia is having its own outbreak of Covid-19. This does not make any sense to me but wait there is a light at the end of the tunnel.

The USA is the modern-day golden fleece, and any kind of illegal activity and or scheme tends to somehow work here in the US of A, be that swindling of older Americans with phone scams or even using people's good nature in bad times, as in stealing of money that was given during any emergency or event, like a hurricane, earthquake or now Covid-19. Mr. Putin now always seems to be able to make money off the USA in deals that the then sitting President cut with and for his true master, the real-life version of the sinister one named Darth Sidious!

This is why Mr. Trumpf (VC) is absolutely the true and real Vladivostok candidate in the flesh, (the one whose name is Abaddon as described in the book of Revelations 9:11, as the Destroyer of **ALL** things). He had to be stopped at all costs on election day at the polls, because this Destroyer has been coerced into working for foreign governments to commit crimes of opportunity against the people of the US on an everyday basis in every way imaginable, both seen and un-seen, to enrich these same said individuals. Sounds like criminal behavior, as in a criminal enterprise to me. Don't ever be fooled! If it walks like a duck, and quakes like a duck, and eats like a duck, then what is it really? Nothing but a duck in my observation.

The Getting Dressed Part:

This whole Covid-19 thing is hard for me because, from my observation, this virus/bacterium appears to be somehow airborne just like the U.S. 82nd and 101st Airborne Rangers Battalions that are stationed in Fort Bragg, North Carolina and Fort Campbell, Kentucky, respectively. That is why the Chinese were air bombing their own cities from the sky with bleach and why everyone in pictures all have on masks to survive this deadly reversed engineered version of the Spanish Influenza (1919) or something close to it. So, if it can live in the air up to 3 hours, that means that it is riding the winds in search of a target of opportunity that it can attack and destroy within 21 days or less. A spit, or a yawn, or a cough or even a choke can be deadly, even just talking to someone can lead to your death. So then, if it is truly in the air and a mask is an essential requirement to aid any human being, then why did the U.S. government say that **NO** masks were even necessary or truly needed, and that proper social distancing (we Americans are in love with the word **SOCIAL** in all its various concepts: social media, Living Social, etc.) would do the trick and should be enough to defeat this invisible enemy. Then if it is in the air and can adhere to most things like metal and clothing or hair or things that are made of plastic, then why did not one person say that it is also vitally important to wear a hat, and have eye covering like glasses, and if possible, cover up whenever you find yourself outside in the open air. People were not even being required to wear gloves and hell (excuse my French) the CDC stated on 03 APR 20 that it required people to wear masks for the very first time. All of this means that staying inside and washing your hands and not ever touching your face or mouth or nose or eyes without washing your hands is not enough on any level. This means that you must always protect yourself, by any means necessary, if you truly want to live a longer life right now. So now dressing the part is just as important as wearing a mask and gloves and therefore getting into the correct or proper behavior modification mindset is crucial. Being aware of how this fast moving and ever-changing situation is from day to day is a must and realize that you can never have too much information as regards this deadly subject matter. I have been wearing a mask since late **FEB 20** and I had worn something to always cover my head when I ventured outside to food shop or to do simple banking and other usual errands like getting a haircut. I had worn two sets of gloves whenever I was outside, with one set being for the outside part, and the second set of inner gloves being the one that I keep on outside of my apartment. I washed with soap or used hand sanitizer just like I would do to my bare hands. Ever since this virus touched down on these shores, I have also kept using my same New Balance sneakers model 520 that are made of plastic that I have continued to use repeatedly and left them strictly outside at the front door to my spot. I never bring my sneakers inside my crib just in case Mr. Covid-19 is on the sneakers somewhere waiting and lurk-ing to kill me or anyone with which it comes into contact. I immediately take a shower as soon as I come inside, and I properly place my clothes that I am wearing in the washing machine to make sure that I am on point as regards safety. So, **ALL** of this may sound like a precautionary tale or somewhat of a germ-a-phobic response to something that no one can see or smell or hear or taste, that had started to kill my fellow American citizens in alarming numbers. But I wanted to live beyond **04 APR 20,** and so getting dressed to go outside and do battle with this sinister opponent was both hard and time consuming to say the very least.

It was like a training exercise where I did the same thing over and over, in a consistent manner, to be ready for what was surely lurking outside that has frightened the whole damn (excuse my French) world. I repeated myself, as best as possible, to modify a behavior that I exhibit that has been engrained into me for the last 30 plus years. But if I wanted to live, then modify I must. No matter if this was just a big hoax to steal the election or to somehow enslave the world into the net of National Socialism, I did not care one damn (excuse my French) bit, because someone must fulfill the role of war correspondent and get the real and true story written. It is just that it took so very long to get dressed to simply go outside in the days of Covid-19, and then it also took just as much time or more to properly undress. As you can read, that simply putting on clothes had become a chore and nuisance, and a safety concern. Please be safe my fellow citizens, and please always stay healthy and stay alive, which means that we should ALWAYS dress the part because the war has truly begun and how you dress for the part, of soldier, could save your life. Resistance is never futile despite what the Borg may say!

Now You JERK Me Down to Sleep:

So here is the thing that I just don't get about Mr. Trumpf, and that is I can see that he is used to jerking people just because he can. I get the concept. Now let me say first, that I am just observing and never ever judging anyone because I don't want anyone judging me. Besides in the United States of America, an opinion and a problem and an asshole, everybody has one. This isn't a diatribe into crying sour grapes, or about racism, or even how things in the United States of America always just seem to be not fair, for c e r t a i n cultural groups, for whatever real reason. Sometimes you must do better to be better, and until you do, you make it easy for people to judge you and your kind, based on your behavior. So, the deal is, that whoever resides at the bottom of any capitalistic structure, will be the ones to get jerked most frequently or hardest. That's right, the bottom rungs of any capitalistic ladder will be jerked or get jerked at every twist and or turn. If you live in the Unites States of America, then it is easy to both know how getting jerked feels and having seen it done many times. Hell (please excuse my French!) this is the United States of America, so for some people getting jerked can either be a lifestyle or for some, so that you can feel better about yourself, or more importantly that you are better than someone else. So, if you think that you are rich, and that most people are beneath you, then just imagine how many fellow citizens that he, number 45 has jerked thus far in his lifetime. He is a dubious businessman, who has taken his father's money, and masterfully with a certain skill and precision made it continue to grow repeatedly, and as such, he has never had a problem jerking people and so-called associates in the name of business and finance.

That is the real art of the deal, which really should be called the thrill of the steal or something catchy like that. There is a basic philosophical question which asks: Why do we do what we do? And the answer is: because we can! Mr. Trumpf has always gotten over on people and used people, and or took advantage of people's kindness and good will. That is just the way that it always has been, simply because he could. He continued to be who he thought that he was, as he grew his brand and celebrity media persona, and somehow stepped into the national and world spotlight to use his guile and deceit to become the President of the United States of America. Kind of like the same thing that George Bush Jr. did when he was able to stumble up on the Presidency for 8 years. But he did not use jerking people in the same manner that Mr. Trumpf always had. Mr. Bush never used it to further his own means to a prefect end.

Okay I still have problems with his **M.O.** (modus of operandi). He was the President, so he should not still have the same behavior patterns and methods of controlling other people. Mr. Trumpf as President was supposed to represent us all, which I know is, laughing out loud, extremely farfetched and illogical, because that just is not how people tend to act when absolute corruptible power is involved. But back to the story, I get it, but he should have just modified his criminal behavior, and jerked everyone else, except us, the actual United States of American citizens. Jerk other countries. Jerk other nations. Jerk other leaders. Jerk the Russian, who is always jerking you (think pulling your chain because he thinks that he is much smarter than you). Jerk The North Korean, who you are shaking bare hands with and who actually looks like he jerks on himself, with that very same hand that you are always shaking (as if a handshake really means something anymore). Hand shaking is out dude because of Covid-19 and don't mean a damn (excuse my French) thing any longer. Perhaps think fist bump. Jerk the Hungarian dude, who out-shined you by using your idea and building a double industrial razor styled fence system to guard his border, and then call it a wall. That is no wall, that is just a barrier or fence that looks like it is keeping some bad ass (excuse my French) prisoners locked away inside. So, jerk him for trying to use your methodology. (Sidenote: the Hungarian just appears to be an arrogant European hole of ass (excuse my French) anyway), Jerk the guy from Turkey, who called you more times per week, than any of the other world leaders ALL combined. And who asked you a gazillion totally unnecessary questions as if he is trying to catch you in either a lie, or to see if you are one of the smartest persons in the world like you claim to anyone who you think is listening! Once again jerk all of them, any nation or country that is not in North America, which means that you also must leave Canada and Mexico alone. They are part of us, so don't never jerk us.

Repeat after me, leave us, and the Canadians and the Mexicans alone comprende? Note: please do not Jerk any of our known allies either: France and the UK and Germany all should get a pass over on any potential Jerking. In retrospect, I think that I should really be giving him the benefit of any doubt, because maybe he just needs some help himself. He could be sick because addictions are classified as a type sickness these days. Maybe he just needs to find a good 12 step program, for jerkers anonymous so that he can deal with his jerking addiction and get into some kind of meaningful recovery program! He just ain't getting it and he needs to recognize that he was not given this wonderful privilege, just for him and his corporation masters and followers to reap all the benefits that go with jerking for sport and money. He said that he wanted to: Make American Great Again but how can you make America great again, if you are jerking the people who make up the American Democracy, as in **WE** the People, in order to form a more perfect Union, etc. Don't forget, to please remember, to JERK the Russian dude before he totally and completely jerks you (which is really the United States of America) and really for what your job title stands for, as if he is better and smarter than you because he lives in Russia, which if my memory serves me right, only stopped being backward about 35 years ago, plus or minus a few years (can I say that?) So in closing : To jerk or not to jerk, that is the real and only question that needs to be both asked and answered of the 45th elected President of these United States of America.

Feeding Yourself During the Covid-19 Days and Times:

Imagine this situation, that the United States which once was the Gold Standard in terms of best nation in the whole wide world, is now just like everywhere else these days and I don't know about you, but for me, myself and I, it is a sad feeling. For United States citizens are standing in line to go into national brand name supermarket stores, and then once finally inside, there are rows and rows of empty shelves for things like toilet paper, or eggs, or beans, or rice, or paper towels, etc. That is a straight up crazy feeling. For here in the United States, food is something that all of us citizens **ALWAYS** take for granted and assumed that it will always and forever be there for the taking, if you have the money that is. So, imagine how everyone is feeling now that we have gotten to this point, and something that we took for granted is now gone or changed into something else. Who stands in line in for food in the United States of America? That is what you see on television that happens in other places in the world, but not here? What the Hell? (excuse my French) Somebody is messing up, in a real way. How is this even happening? Right how? Food? We are talking about standing in a line 6 feet apart from the next person that is in the front and back of you, and then when you get inside the store itself, what you are there to get is not there. The space is empty. It is no national holiday like Thanksgiving or Christmas, or the 4th of July, or New Years Day. People appear to be terrorized by all this media inspired sensationalism, and rightly so, and it is like the end of the world is coming, and food hording has become the norm and not the exception like it used to be. This part of the Covid 19 Wars is subtle and a below the surface kind of mental takedown. This affects the human brain on so many different levels because it involves different things like terror, fear, helplessness, and hopelessness. It is like 9/11 everyday, all day, all the time. It feels a lot like you are not able to ever let your guard down nor should you, and it becomes a daily grind to survive our circumstance that we find ourselves. Then on top of just about everything else, throw in the lack of food and this Covid-19 War suddenly becomes more heart stopping. I am what you call an American, and we do things that are based upon our own selfish desires, whims and wants. We all talk a great game but, for most of us, our hearts, minds and souls are just not into anything remotely harder challenging. Anything that requires thinking and planning is off the table, and we have no work ethic or sense of doing the right thing for the right reason at the right time. So, standing in a line to get some food is way below everyone's mental pay grade and besides, it feels like we are in some third world county.

A Funny Story:

The smartest person in the whole wide world: There is a plane with 5 passengers on board. Donald Trumpf, Dr. Anthony Fauci, the Pope,

Hillary Clinton, and a 10-year-old schoolgirl. Something happens and the plane is about to crash and there are only 4 parachutes. Dr. Fauci said I need one to help develop the cure for Covid-19. He took one and jumped out of the plane. The Pope then says, I need one so I can help spiritually guide people through this health crisis. He took one and jumped out of the plane. Mr. Trumpf said I am the smartest person in the USA, and he takes one and jumps out of the plane. Hillary Clinton says to the 10-year-old schoolgirl, you take the last one. I have lived my life and your just getting started with yours. The 10 year-old schoolgirl says don't worry because there are 2 parachutes left. The smartest man in the world took my book bag!

Can You Say Leadership?

There is a saying that great leaders are born to lead, while everyone else is born to follow. Great leaders are both respected and admired for their ability to lead the masses and do so in an effective manner. Ask any group of assembled people for attributes of leadership, and I am sure that you will hear common or similar things, like well read, intelligent, smart, introspective, charismatic, savvy, etc., to describe a person. Most people will immediately focus on people in positions of authority, but you can also be a leader in any type of job, team, company, friendship group, or even a family structure. Leadership is not confined to one's sex or skin color or religious affiliation. Most leaders are smart and have what is called the "it" factor, which personally I call presence. They just have this command thing (as in naturally being in command example: General Colin Powell) about themselves and they also have a certain amount of thought leadership that just oozes out from the core of their very being. Leaders also respond in times of need or whenever there is a crisis or event that requires their particular skill set. Leaders also make no excuses, and they also have a certain amount of grit and determination to get any job done despite the cost or personal sacrifice. Hard times also bring people with leadership qualities to the front of the line, as they step up to meet their destinies and discover who they truly are for the greater good. I say that because I need you to know that in the context of what I am about to say that I am not about to judge anyone; these are strictly my very own personal observations when I say that history will show that Mr. Trumpf who became the 45th President of the United States of America is no true leader. He is smart, and devious, and he was able to capture the seat of the Presidency, but he has no real or defined leadership skills. First, he is a businessman and not a politician, therefore he has no rules or set of previously defined practices that guide his behavior patterns. He has no real values other than the drive for acquiring money and wealth. This drive is also not integrity based upon solid principles that are both valid and reliable.

He is also not very good about controlling his emotions, and so he tends to strike back at anyone who questions his so-called authority. All of which points to the fact that he has never acted presidential in any kind of public setting that requires him to speak out or field questions. He also has a certain amount of vanity, as evidenced by his hair, and instead of him wearing his glasses whenever he must read anything, like a prepared speech, he stumbles through everything as if he cannot read, which is evident by the fact that he always must look down and never up at the audience the whole time that he is reading something. He can read, he just cannot see very well without his glasses, and if he is so smart like he thinks that he is because he was able to accomplish this massive feat of becoming the President, then why not wear some contacts so that he does not take away from his look of perfection that he is **ALWAYS** trying to project. **Go figure?**

He has this innate need to be liked or always believed, when really, he is both mean and nasty and condescending to anyone who opposes him or his reckless make it up as you go along agenda. He is a reckless and dishonest businessman, and a lot of his business qualities he has transitioned over to his newest job, even though the job title seems to imply goodness and truth, and more importantly doing the right thing for the right reason. But this is a person who has rejected the established protocols, and he appears only to be using the office of the President to further his own selfish desires of acquiring mo money mo money while in office which is a serious conflict of interest. Most men who have been President at least wait until their terms are over to take a wade in the money pool, but he is using his "steal as much as you can business model", to perfection and self-enrichment. He also has this look or attitude that he thinks that he is better than most people in the United States or the world, and thus he is unable to relate to 95 % of the people in this country. But just because you have a lot of money and Power doesn't make you any better than anyone else. He thinks that he is, but his legacy as a businessperson has already tarnished the office of the Presidency. He is the one in his early years who put the terrible attacking and pre-judging advertising in the NY Times newspaper for $85,000.00 about the Central Park 5, who eventually were found not guilty. He is also the one who has bankrupted numerous companies, and never given a red cent to save any of the employees. He is the one who has bilked people of money, time and time again, so he did not have to pay them for their services rendered on job sites. He is the one who banks would not give any more loans to because he always defaults on the loan, as if the banks were giving to him and only him, free money. He is the one who does not want to disclose his tax filings because he does not want anyone to know his true wealth, which I have always believed was much lower than he states or spouts off in public. So, in all honesty does he have the qualities and or attributes of what our past leaders have always had? Is he a leader or is he a reckless follower of the real rich people in this county that are known as the 1 %? Is he the kind of person that you would even want to follow? If there was ever a serious crisis in this country, is he the one that you would listen to for any kind of guidance or instructions? Note: If I had to vote, right now for a presidential candidate and or a leader based upon leadership qualities and all-around moxie, it would be either, Governor Cuomo (NY), Governor Newsom (CA), Governor Whitmer (MI), Governor Hogan (MD), and Mayor Bowser of the Federal District of Columbia, Mayor Lance-Bottoms of Atlanta GA and then Joe Biden.

03 May 2020 Death tolls:

Washington DC: 240 Deaths/ 666 Recovered / 4,797 confirmed

United States: 67,067 Deaths/ 152,000 Recovered/ 1.16 million confirmed

Worldwide: 244,000 Deaths/ 1.1 million Recovered/ 3.44 million confirmed

The Curious Case of the Missing Face Masks?

So, some people are not wearing masks at all, and they are the very same ones who are protesting and storming the state Capitals in certain states because they want to stop the state-imposed detention, think lockdown, and go back to work and partake in what folks call social behaviors (example Restaurants, Bars, Clubs, etc.). Seriously this whole thing is perplexing because if something can be in the air that can kill you is floating all about, then why would you not have a mask on? The pictures from **ALL** around the entire planet show people with masks on or any other type of face covering on and I assume that they have them on because they want to **LIVE,** and really get on the other side of this pandemic situation still breathing and eating and being a human. So why are certain citizens of these (so called) United States of America acting like their constitutional rights are at risk? (The Don't Tread On Me types) What changed their attitudes?

I really think that this whole thing is back to that elephant that has always been in the room, here in all mighty US of A, race relations. They truly have never been accurately addressed since the end of the Civil War back in 1865. Race relations are at an all-time low right about now which is evident with the increasing numbers of murders that are occurring with a racial twist to them. Certain data was strategically released in a report by the CDC on April 8th, 2020, to show the specified infection and death rates by race, which meant to highlight the fact that Black citizens were dramatically overrepresented among Covid 19 patients that were sick enough to be hospitalized. Then almost overnight, that changed the face of the pandemic into a Black situation. Then 5 days later April 13, 2020, a small group of angry and armed protesters, who were White and mostly not wearing masks, gathered in front of the Ohio statehouse to demand that Governor DeWine reopen the state. Then from North Carolina to Texas more protesters gathered, with the assistance of right-wing organizers and supported by Republican legislators, until on April 30th, 2020, the protesters in Michigan tried to storm and push their way into the Statehouse but were repelled by the Statehouse security forces. All of this because Covid-19 appears to be a Black folk's killer, and only affects Black people and not anyone else, even though Black people are considered a minority in this country. Because if Blacks only constitute somewhere hovering around 12 to 14% of the population of the USA, yet 28% of the Covid 19 cases in the US are Black citizens, then sadly most random citizens would falsely assume that if they were not Black, then it is not going to affect them. This is flawed thinking folks because everyone can do the math right? 100 minus 28 is what? Oh yeah 72% non-Black who have Covid-19 cases. So please do not be fooled into riding on that elephant that is **ALWAYS** in the room, here in the U.S., as regards race and race relations.

The real question is why is it killing Black citizens like that? I feel that it is because Covid-19 is killing people who interact with one another, and a lot of Black citizens in this country have fought and marched and sang (think We Shall Overcome) and fought and danced and entertained to have those kinds of participating jobs that are both secure and needed to make our Great Society work. Participating jobs are the jobs that allow you to participate in the American society or dream, on some level, that gives the false narrative of the middle-class illusion that you are a full citizen of this Great Society, even though you know deep down inside of your heart that you will never be fully accepted no matter how much money, fame or fortune you are able to acquire. So, ambulance drivers, morticians, bus drivers, janitors, Post Office employees, firemen, police officers, nurses, factory workers, cooks, bank tellers, grocery store employees, schoolteachers, beauticians, the list goes on and on, all interact with fellow citizens in a up close and personal manner.

So Covid 19 is really killing its victims by job description and not by race per say, which is what our current national leadership is not accurately saying. The flames of race hatred are being fanned to promote ignorance and stupidity and getting re-elected. **Remember that dumbness can be hereditary, but stupidity is always a choice.** To my fellow citizens please, pretty please with a cherry on top don't be stupid about Covid 19 because Covid 19 is killing all colors, all religions, all age groups (depending upon where you live in the world that is) all nationalities, all creeds, all cultures, all human Genotypes. It is not killing primarily only one race of people nor is it not going to affect you just because you are of another racial classification. Covid 19 can strike down anyone who catches it, and it can also amplify any previous or existing condition into a death sentence. Just because you seem healthy you may not be, all of which creates a lot of self-doubt and second guessing yourself, which ultimately can lead to terror and fear.

So always wear a mask, and never think that money or opening the economy to save your jobs, are worth more than your life. If you are dead than how can you work the job, but I live here so I get it, and completely understand why you think that your way of life is being threatened and why it is so very important to you and your fellow patriots to "Make America Great Again". For you have been neglected for far too long, and in America where everyone has an origin story, yours has been conveniently forgotten, or dismissed. You have every right to protest anything that you feel is threatening your Constitutional Rights, in your pursuit of life, liberty and happiness. But if you are dead because of some very flawed thinking, then what good does that do for you? Remember that dumbness can be hereditary, but stupidity is always a choice, so all that I am passionately asking is just for everyone to stay better informed, so that everyone can make better choices. I end with a quote from Oscar Wilde: "Imitation is the sincerest form of flattery that mediocrity can pay to greatness".

.

The Original 13 Colonies and Covid-19

The original 13 colonies were Massachusetts Bay, Delaware, Pennsylvania, New Jersey, New York, Georgia, Connecticut, Maryland, North Carolina, South Carolina, New Hampshire, Virginia and the Federal District of Columbia, making those 16 distinct areas. As of **17 April 2020, 21,851** citizens of United States who live the total area of the original 13 Colonies have died thus far and this makes the area of the original 13 Colonies the hardest hit area of the United States on a whole. This is interesting because most people assumed that the west coast region of the U.S. would be the hardest hit area of the country due the proximity to the Pacific Ocean and Asia. But the majority of the Covid 19 cases that helped to spread the virus did not come from Asia. It ever so sneakily came from Europe on airplanes, from tourist friendly places like Spain and Italy, and even though Seattle Washington was at first thought to be the original ground zero city and state. This would make it to have higher numbers than anywhere else.

The Original 13 Colonies became the leader in infections and deaths. The Original 13 Colonies area has major cities like New York City, Boston, Philadelphia, Pittsburg, Raleigh-Durham, Washington DC, Atlanta, Annapolis, Stamford, Hartford, Albany, Syracuse, Buffalo, Rochester, Portland ME, Trenton, Wilmington DE, Charlotte, Baltimore and Richmond VA, all of which have high numbers of infections and deaths. These cities also contribute heavily to the economy of the US and provide the entire nation with vitally important education and technology centers that keep the United States moving and thus growing each day. What would the framers of the Constitution have thought about how the sitting United States President has done as regarding protection of the Original **13** colonies? Would they have approved of his behavior and saw through the smoke screen of him wanting and needing to get re-elected over the lives of the very same citizens that he swore in an oath to protect? Why has he made certain things essential services like liquor stores, or McDonald's hamburger joints, and home or office building construction crews, and never said, in the beginning of all this that church was one of the most essential services of **ALL**?

Why has he only helped certain states based upon the political party that the governors are aligned with, and has repeatedly lied about wanting to help when he is really a major part of the overall problem because of his actions and spoken words? Why has he promoted getting paid (creating a U.S. based vaccine) and stealing money (trying to control the patent of any vaccine) more important than the very lives of each and every citizen of this Great Experiment that is called the United States of America? Why has he not done everything possible to protect and defend the people that the very Constitution speaks of, (**WE** the people in order to form) in a more vigorous manner of leadership and determination? What would or could be more important than the lives of our still young nation's, citizens themselves?

Did the oath that he took on the very day that he was inaugurated mean nothing more than the words on a piece of paper? Well personally, I think that they would have had no other choice but to see him as a tyrant, the exact same kind of tyrant that they were desperately trying to get away from and be rid of, back in their time period, who was called the Great King of England.

The Antifa Swindle:

Antifa is a term that stands for Anti-Fascist, and it is not an organization nor some kind of group and there is no membership, nor is there any kind of leader. The protesters have used this term in their protest signs to only cut down on having to spell out the word Anti-Fascist. Now somehow strangely the current sitting US President, Donald J Trumpf has become convinced that Antifa is a terrorist organization, and has branded them one, and placed Antifa on the domestic terrorist watch list. Besides the basic Captain Obvious question, of what the hell (excuse my French)? is a more pressing and important one that I need answered, which is, who doesn't like anti fascists and who isn't hell (excuse my French) bent to totally get rid of them? The one who does not like an anti-fascist has to be a fascist him or herself. Anti-fascist is the opposite of fascist, so why then is a term considered a domestic terrorist organization?

The Photo Opportunity:

On **June 1, 2020,** after a peaceful protest outside of Lafayette Park, the sitting United States Attorney General, Mr. William Barr, stated that they needed the battle space, in front of the White House, dominated so that they could move the perimeter of the peaceful protest march some two blocks away.

Because the night before, the fake me out protesters had turned violent and began a series of unlawful civil disobedience and looted businesses, then burned cars and numerous trash cans and orange parking cones, and then threw 1 brick and over 100 bottles of water at the U.S. Secret Service Police who were guarding the fence of the White House. These rioters had even come close to breeching the gates of the White House, so close that the President and his wife Melania and son Barron all had to take an elevator ride down into the nuclear bomb proof bunker for their safety. These rioters had also set a church on fire, even though the bishop of that very same church had sided with the protestors and had given them food and water and a place to rest and use the bathroom in the very same church. For the life of me, I cannot seem to figure out why would they set it on fire when it was aiding their cause?

The very next night is when the President during a speech at 6:45 PM in the Rose Garden stated that he was the law-and-order President and before 7:00 PM a disperse order was to take effect. He and Mr. Barr sicked the National Guard and elements of the 82nd Airborne Division on the protesters with a very disturbing show of force, using both tear gas and rubber bullets to dominate the battle space that has filled with peaceful U.S. citizens mind you, so that President Trump could then walk across the street to the front of the church and take a photo of himself holding up a Bible that looked at first like it was upside down, as if to show the world that he was the real law-and-order President. Then to add insult to injury, he then boasted about it, when really it was Mr. Barr's doing, even though the President tried to take credit for the shameful misuse of power. What U.S. President has ever used forced force against peaceful U.S. citizens when there was no war?

Does the Attorney General of the U.S. have the authority to order military troops to attack U.S. citizens and then say that what he did pertained to the Insurrection Act of 1850? 1850! Come on now, sadly although we have seen just how determined that Mr. Trumpf is to trample on the rights of any and all U.S. citizens who do not look or think like him. It is even more disturbing to see how many people are also going along with him as he dismantles democracy and freedom of speech. Democracy always dies in darkness ladies and gentlemen. They want you to think that it is about gun rights and allegiance to the flag when they do not respect anyone's First Amendment rights except their own. Who are they really trying to kid here? The common criminals who are looting and using the protest to cover their tracks are no better than the President and his cronies, who are twisting the narrative, to make it fit, a model of their own choosing. So always remember my fellow citizens that two wrongs never make a right.

The Stimulus Check Blues

The United States of America's economy took a serious nose down down-turn, once the governors of each state locked the states down, to help keep the numbers of Covid 19 related deaths down, by making sure that social distancing was in place. A lot of citizens who had those certain jobs that deal with many people daily began to fill the crunch of the loss of jobs and wages. Soon after anywhere between 8 to 12 weeks without pay, a lot of people were in serious trouble and seeking assistance or bail out or handout or whatever you want to call it, to help them get through the maddening situation. The Federal Government finally stepped up to help members of society, and proposed a bail out to assist the people of democracy because after all it is **WE** the people and not **WE** the corporations. After our political leadership haggled and argued over the situation, and both members of Congress decided that enough was enough, they finally came up with $1,200.00 dollars, that was to go to the average citizens who fell below a certain level of annual income, even though in many countries around the world the average citizens were given much more. (Example Canada)

A stimulate the economy package was designed to help businesses and people of the Great Society because everyone was affected by the downturn in the economy. The bewildering part was that the corporations got paid first out of the stimulus package while only few actual citizens received anything. The excuse was that the people who had already paid their taxes naturally were the first to receive, even though the Commander in Chief gave an extension on the drop-dead tax date 15 April, which made people not in the slightest rush to file because they were looking for the stimulus money of $1,200. So began the stimulus blues game, where everyone who really needed the money was not seeing any check nor a direct deposit into their bank into their bank accounts. Back and forth this maddening game went, with more and more excuses being given just each and every day as to where the checks were, as citizens got deeper and deeper into debt waiting for something that seemed not to come. Then after 8 weeks, on Thursday June 25th came the news that over 1 million dead people had received checks by account mistake! **MISTAKE?** How can dead people receive checks when people who are alive and in need still receive nothing? Why would someone even send a check to a dead person, and what kind of person would you have to be, to even devise such a cruel and cold-hearted act? That was like a slap in the face to the needy. Then they had the nerve and unmitigated gall to tell folks to send them back, as in return to sender, if you received one that was addressed to a dead loved one!

Okay America, this should be time to wake up call to action. Whose country is this? Democracy means people, not like a plutocracy which means a few and the people running things are doing their best to sell us a bill of fake goods, while they run the country into the ground and steal as much as they possibly can in the name of making America great again. The missing stimulus check of $1,200 could have helped 1 million United States families in a real way, yet this was just sadly another carefully designed tactic to create more frustration and keep people mentally down. The further that folks can be pushed downwards, then it will take many more years to recover, if recovery is even possible.

A lot of American people have already lost everything, and the making of America into a debtor nation only truly serves for one purpose, and that is if you can make the greatest nation in the world, the United States of America bend to its knees, then liberty and justice around the world will suffer. Then who will come to the aid of nations in the world who really need help. The USA has a history of rescuing nations that are in need, for whatever reason, be that by a natural disaster or puppet regimens for liberty and justice and freedom. This is what this is all about, to cut the United States of America and its helping hands off from the rest of the world, which only serves to further the would-be dictators and despots in places like Russia, Brazil, North Korea, Philippines, Saudi Arabia, etc. as they seek absolute control in their countries with no one to check the advance of their authoritarian style of government.

How can we help the world, if we are not able to help our own citizens by giving them $1,200 from one of the world's richest treasuries which as well over a trillion dollars in it? The Commander in Chief helped Russia but not our own citizens. People of the United States can anyone please explain to us all, how was this truly making America great again? Good luck on that one.

Is it me or what? 02 July 20

I am sitting inside looking out of a window and wondering is it me or can anyone see what is truly happening? Things seem normal, but they are not, and you even hate to turn on the television set because you will be bombarded with images of the Covid 19 war, with death totals, science facts and figures, Covid 19 stories that seem designed to strike fear and doom and gloom within the average and everyday citizens. First, on or around May 1st, 2020, there was a big stink to open back up the states to restart the economy. The citizens of Michigan caused a no mask wearing revolt, because the media had made the virus seem like it was only affecting certain members of our great society. Therefore, the Commander in Chief used this ruckus as a means to an end, to endorse opening the USA when it was clearly way too early to do so. But a certain political party let states seemed to be listening to the Commander in Chief and his rhetoric when they should have used caution and restraint and just waited a few weeks longer despite what their constituents thought was good for them.

Sadly, states with Republican governors like Florida, Georgia, Texas, and Arizona that opened back up early, were hit the hardest with the Covid 19 virus, and why did no one say that these governors were to blame for following the advice of the Commander in Chief? The Democrats seemed mighty determined to take the high road and not bash or belittle the commander in Chief when he bashed them at least twice every day. Why did they not speak the truth, and let folks know that the rise in the Covid 19 numbers were directly tied to the Commander in Chief's resistance to re-open the economy so that he could get re-elected? This is a man who had no problem taking credit for other people's triumphs and victories, and he would never say that he made a mistake in judgement in any decisions or point of view that he espoused. For example, he wanted there to be less testing, when if he were a real President of and for the people, he would have immediately insisted upon nationwide mandatory door to door testing to take place, and not make it voluntary.

Even more crazy was his insistence that no one had to wear masks, which is vital to stop or slow the spread of the Covid 19 virus everywhere else in the world except here in the United States of America. That does not make sense, but I am just one citizen with only 1 vote, so what do I truly know? In hindsight, the opening back up early was clearly a judgement call that was not based upon anything sound or rational. The science was telling everyone that an early opening could have disastrous consequences, and in some States things got worse. He may have wanted folks to die or be afraid in the first place, so that this thing would get sideways and affect the election in November 2020.

The numbers speak for themselves and can't be denied: (see below)

July 02, 2020: Covid 19 numbers:

USA 2.74 million cases (+ 52,609) with 130,000 deaths
Worldwide 10.7 million cases (+ 172,000) with 516,000 deaths
Florida 169,000 cases (+ 6563) with 3, 617 deaths (+45)
Texas 169,000 cases (+8016) with 2481 deaths (+57)
Georgia 84, 237 cases (+2946) with 2827 deaths (+ 22)
Arizona 84, 092 cases (+4877) with 1720 deaths (+88)

Then throw in Ohio 2876 deaths (+13) and Alabama 947 deaths (+21) a South Carolina 766 deaths (+37) and you can see that all the Republican led states had serious problems as regards containment of the virus.

Instead of getting to a better place after 4 months, the nation had some bad hot spots that got worse before they got better. All of this was because the Commander in Chief refused to value human lives over his re-election bid, and the consequences of his actions were a death sentence for some people when there was no real reason for any of this.

Instead of M.A.G.A. it should really be spelled M.R.G.A.

It is July 11, 2020, and the pandemic is raging full blown out of control in certain states (Arizona, Florida, Georgia, South Carolina, and Texas) while the President #45 seeks to re-open the schools and get re-elected so that he can do four more years of this kind of often hate inspired rhetoric. During his election in 2016, he coined the phrase Make America Great Again, as if somehow the United States of America had taken a fall from its lofty perch and was no longer the world leader that is has always been. That somehow all the progress that we had made as a country by 8 years of the previous Obama administration had been undone, and that he was here to settle the score and return the nation to its proper greatness. You saw the red baseball hats with M. A. G. A. embolden on them everywhere and the term M. A. G. A. became synonymous with supporting of Mr. Trumpf. People from every walk and way of life used their 1st Amendment rights to proudly show who they were voting for, and the term M. A. G. A. became a flash point of conversation just about everywhere that you went. But three and a half years later, it appeared that M. A. G. A. was a ruse, and really was not a symbol of racism or closed and erratic thinking but really stood for something else. It really stood for M. R. G. A., or Making Russia Great Again, and this is whom Mr. Trumpf is truly supporting and ultimately bowing down to, as he takes a knee for Russian interests and hegemony.

He is helping to create a new wanna be world leader, even though Russia and its interests are only about Russia. Russia provides no aid and support for nations who are in need, nor does Russia promotes health initiatives and financial aid to anyone but Russia. Russia is a bully. Look at Ukraine and the Chechen state or province within Russia. It has never ever tried to be anything else than what it is. Russia needs a weakened USA so that it can expand beyond its natural borders. Past USA Presidents understood this fact and always kept an eye on Russia and its movements to keep it in check, so to speak. Russia has played 2nd fiddle in the concert of life this whole time, and it is now tired of this role. It appears that it now wants to become the 1st fiddle in the concert. Always remember that Russia signed a non-aggression pact with Germany in the 30's and they were considered an ally until Germany blindsided them and attacked them in the 40's during World War 2. So, because of this Russia trusts no one be that friend or foe.

For it is not like Russia was some world class nation, it just had remarkable and family loving people who are able to withstand the cruelty of the elements and survive despite the odds. Russia produces nothing world changing, no technology, no science or math or engineering or medical advancements, no nothing; just great vodka and sexy no hold barred women, which in most cases is not going to change the world in any remarkable manner. Russia needs the nation that is the true and undisputed leader of the so-called free world (USA) to be in disarray so that it can continue its march towards world domination. Russia is a taker, not a giver and that is exactly what Mr. Trumpf is also. He too in most cases is a user and abuser, as if by being able to take something from someone shows that he is stronger or somehow better than the victim. Sounds like the perfect Webster's dictionary definition of the work bully to me. For Russia to grow, it needs assistance from Mr.

Trumpf, which is why Russia meddled in the 2016 Presidential election boys and girls. Russia's leadership knew that the U.S. with Mr. Trumpf as the president and at the helm, is a weakened U.S. The hoodwink is that when you see people proudly wearing their M. A. G. A. hats, it really means M. R. G. A.: Make Russia Great Again plain and simple.

It would not even surprise me if Mr. Trumpf would have used Russia to invade the USA, because he lost the election, to rescue him in his time of need. His loss meant he claimed that he was cheated, and the only world class powers that would ever step in and be big and bad would-be Russia, because Mr. Trumpf has done everything in his power to make Russia great again, even though it never ever was so great in the first place. So, think about that every time you see someone wearing those fake me our M. A. G. A. hats with an enormous amount of pride and self- serving hypocrisy.

In closing thank you for your support and reading effort and always remember that Lady Democracy is dying. She is bleeding out. She ain't dead yet, but she could very well die if we as a nation do not seek out the truth. Maybe the Democrats should start making and selling and wearing blue baseball hats with M. R. G. A stitched on the front to settle the odds. No, that would be a dirty and against the rules, so they would never fight a fire with a stronger fire, which always plays into Republicans and others' thinking. He knew that Covid 19 was dangerous, but he wanted to downplay everything. The great writer Bob Woodward has written a book about the 45th Commander in Chief that is titled 'Rage'. In this book, the Commander in Chief openly stated on tape that he knew since February 2020, about the effects of Covid 19, but he really wanted to downplay the whole thing as to not to cause a panic. A panic, not wanting to cause a panic. If he did not want to cause a panic, then why did he state that masks were not required for an airborne pathogen? Panic, then why was he not concerned with U.S. citizens lives, and he could have saved many people. He really wanted to use Covid to only further his agenda to get re-elected and create a panic on voting day so that citizens would be more concerned with living than about voting. This would help to serve his true cause of getting re-elected so that he could get 4 more years of ruining this once great country with his brand of destruction and mayhem.

This omission was particularly troubling because it only goes to show just how twisted he really is to achieve his own means to an end. U.S. citizens lives mean nothing to him, because back in May he stated that it is the way that it is, regarding people dying from the effects of Covid 19. Therefore, he wanted people to die which is troubling because as the President have not you taken an oath to protect and serve the American people? This is supposed to be a democracy for the people, but letting people die is cruel and inhumane. He also appears to only care for his base, which has elements of National Socialism and bigotry all intertwined together to form an imperfect union. So let everyone else die and just stay focused on his base and making America great again.

The greatness of America is not what we used to be, but ultimately in what we are to become. The greatness of America is that, yes, we started as a great experiment and this experiment although not perfect was a start towards something new and profound. This experiment was to create a more perfect union, where everyone could prosper and live a dream of their own making and choice. Sure, it has been a constant battle to see who runs or is in control of the experiment, but if everyone had a good life and money was there for the taking, then it was a win-win situation. But to participate in the murder of U.S. citizens by doing nothing and using misinformation and fake me out news to further a political agenda that a businessman now wants to rely upon is downright unfathomable to com- prehend. The Commander in Chief is not a true politician in any sense of the word. He is a true dyed in the wool only-for-profit businessman with his only goal to re-capturing the highest office in the land so that he and the ones who are participating with him can benefit while Covid 19 continues to kill people every day.

Sept 18, 2020

The Death of an Icon: Supreme Court Justice Ruth Bader-Ginsberg died in the evening at her home surrounded by her much beloved family members. With her passing the Commander in Chief had a chance to replace his 3rd Justice to the highest court in the land. Justice Bader-Ginsberg fought a remarkable fight against cancer, and had vowed to stay around, as in alive, until after the 2020 Presidential election. But she passed away with few days left. Justice Bader-Ginsberg was a true Icon and national treasure that simply cannot be replaced. She was a symbol for all women that a woman is just as equal to a man, and in some cases better, and that as a woman you should never let anyone define who you are or more importantly what you should or could be. Her death kicked off a tremendous battle in this country to get another conservatively right centered individual placed upon the court to swing the votes back towards the dark ages. Then a lot of laws are going to change to reflect a more conservative viewpoint, and this will ultimately in the end, only serve to affect diversity and free speech and liberty and the pursuit of happiness. Instead of God bless America, it really should be God Pray for America.

The Election Drama

The election came on November 3rd, 2020, and the Biden/ Harris team won, but there was so much hocus pocus and back and forth leading up to it that the Trump/Pence team caused, that they had a chance to win/steal the election despite what the U.S. citizens voted. They screwed up the mail so that the voter mail in process would be slowed way down. They kept talking about voter fraud, and they let the Covid 19 situation go so that it would affect the outcome for them. 70 million plus people voted for them, but 75 million plus voted for the Biden/ Harris team. Strangely Trump continued to state that he had won? That he had been cheated and that things were rigged against him. Clearly, he was lying but what was his true endgame?

Well, he is slick, and all that he was doing was to get more contributions to a Super Pac that he had created, under the guise of voter recounts (which cost money because they are done all by hand) to drum up enough money to go towards his 442-million-dollar tax bill that the **U.S. Southern**

District of New York State Attorney's Office says that he owes on a delinquent tax bill. He is supposed to share 40 % of the funds that are in the Pac with the Republican Party, but he is a crook and is trying to stay out of jail starting on the 21 January 2021. He has been dragging everything out even though by Saturday 07 NOV 20 the election results were officially in, and he had been declared the **LOSER** (he gets the L).The 45th President has been adamant that he won an election that he officially lost because of his behavior to be able to siphon off enough of money, so that he can stay out of jail and act as if he and his rule has been both just and honorable. He is most certainly a Wiley T. Coyote type of individual who feeds upon the weak and scared to further his own selfish goal of dominating all battle fields. Thank God almighty that he and his minions lost the election, because I do not know if the U.S. of America and the entire world for that matter could have survived 4 more years under #45 and his people.

As of July 2022

Number 45 loses the Nov 2020 election to Joe Biden, but claims that he actually won, because of so called voter fraud in certain key states where he had expected to win as he had done in the 2016 election, even though he and his staff knew that he had lost. All the states that he claimed fraud in (Georgia, Pennsylvania, Arizona, etc.) double and triple checked the results, and they all found that **NO FRAUD** had ever occurred. Then on 06 January 2021, on the day of the votes being certified by Congress, Number 45 has a suspicious rally/ protest. After the rally/ protest he directed the people in attendance to go up on Capitol Hill and protest the certification of the election results. When the protestors got to the US Capital building, they start committing acts of sedition and treason (think Benedick Arnold) against the Constitution and the rule of law, as they forcefully broke into and then stormed the U.S. Capital building. When everything was settled, this treasonous action resulted in the death of 4 Capitol Hill police along with 4 protesters, with the U.S. Capital building defaced and vandalized by angry everyday U.S. citizens.

These acts seemed to pose a serious threat to democracy itself. It looks like democracy and the actual Constitution in this republic for which it stands are both now in dangerous situations, as the Republic struggles to remain alive and thrive. Despite false rumors of another uprising, The U.S. of America does have a peaceful transition of power on inauguration day.

What else? The Supreme Court!
The Supreme Court of the United States, which is the highest court in the land, was gifted 3 people onto the court by # 45 (Trump), and this was done to change or sway the balance of liberal thought and rulings to make the Court swing back hard to the right of the center line. On **June 21, 2022**, the Supreme Court ruled that a Maine program that excludes religious schools from a state tuition program is a violation of the free exercise of religion (think separation of church and state).

First on **June 23, 2022**, the Supreme Court ruled that receiving your Miranda warning isn't technically a protected Constitutional right any longer. A Miranda warning "you have the right to remain silent, and anything that you say can and will be used against you in a court of law". Protection from the 5th Amendment supposedly still remains but the police will no longer be subject to civil lawsuit if they fail to give you this warning. It just means that law enforcement no longer must inform people that they have this right. People supposedly still will have this right, but if they then that is your responsibility, for you as a citizen of this Republic should know the laws, more importantly you can't sue law enforcement, or get the case thrown out due to law enforcement not properly doing their jobs in the very first place. Then again on **June 23, 2022,** the Supreme Court ruled that states with strict laws on carrying guns in public violates the 2nd Amendment. So now you can carry your gun or guns in public, all of which simply does away with laws or procedures that enforce gun owners to adhere to certain rules regarding guns in public.

On **June 24, 2022,** the Supreme Court ruled that banning nearly all abortions after 15 weeks of pregnancy is unconstitutional, (which throws this issue back to the actual State level). overturned the Roe v Wade law which had been in place for over 50 plus years. Which opened the door for all kinds of so-called trigger laws to be enacted in a lot of states or on the state level. On **June 27, 2022,** the Supreme Court ruled that a football coach at a public high school had a constitutional right to pray at the 50-yard line. On **June 29, 2022** the Supreme Court ruled that state authorities may prosecute non-Indians who commit crimes against Indians on those reservations. This goes against the sovereignty of Indian lands, plain and simple. On **June 30, 2022,** the Supreme Court ruled that the EPA's (Environmental Protection Agency) ability to regulate the energy sector is now limited to emission controls at individual power plants, thus in effect stripping the EPA of the power that the U.S. Congress gave it, to respond to the most pressing environmental challenges of our modern times.

Note: There have been 1148 mass shootings in the US ever since Covid began, where a mass shooting is defined as 4 or more people. In 2019 211 shootings, in 2020 281 shootings, in 2021 342 shootings and in 2022 (as of JULY 11, 2022) 314 shootings with roughly 6 more months to go in the 2022 calendar year.

The True Survival Manual · 57

Epilogue (Ep.l.loge) : A section or speech at the end of a book or play, that serves as a comment or a conclusion to what has happened.

Covid 19 statistics as of 30 AUG 23

Global: Confirmed: 769,805,366 and Deaths: 6,955,484 with Brazil @ 704,659 and India @531,925 and Russia@ 399,938 and Mexico @ 334,336 and United Kingdom @ 228,707 and Peru @ 221, 364 as the highest totals besides The United States of America

National: Confirmed 103,436,829 and Deaths: 1,127,152 with California @ 102,356, and Texas@ 92,378 and Florida@ 89,075 and New York @77,423 and Pennsylvania @ 51,344 and Georgia @ 42,351 and Ohio@ 42,299 and Illinois @ 39,381 and New Jersey @ 35,774 and Arizona @ 29,852 and Indiana @ 25,959 and Virgina@ 23,769 (and the Federal District of Columbia @ 1,392)

Commander in Chief Number 45-

4 indictments, and 91 total number of criminal charges in 4 separate cases, in a direct attempt to go against the Constitution which he had taken an sworn oath to protect, as the leader of the United States of America as if his sworn allegiance meant nothing but a means to an end to achieve his desired results. He then used dirty tricks and 6 tactics to try to maintain power, and they were: Big lies or ideas, misinformation and disinformation, dependency of his allies, marginalization of all opponents, dividing and conquering of all foes and even friends, along with violence or threats of violence. He attacked foes and friends, and he used the so called party of Lincoln, the Republican party in a way that had never ever been

thought of before to continue his autocratic hold or grip. He seems to process a surprisingly odd sense of justice that seems to only benefit his benefactors, and he also more importantly wants to leave his autocratic mark upon the United states as well as the world that would last long after he has passed on or transitioned onward. So if he had to use violence or a treat of violence to get his way, then so be it, and really it appears that it honestly made him no matter, because no matter what happened , he could and would use his position, to get amnesty under the Presidential Immunity clause, because somehow or in some way the rules of the Great Experiment doesn't apply to him (just as he views paying taxes) .

So, because of his ingrained and treasonous behavior (think modus operandi), over 1000 people (citizens) who willingly participated in the 06 Jan revolt, have been charged with federal crimes, and 623 people have been adjudicated and 378 individuals have been sentenced to periods of incarceration. **(as of 25 SEP 23)** But the really sad part is that many of our fellow citizens, especially certain ones who are politicians, have been co-conspirators with all of the lies and more importantly have been complicit in the lies and deceit, and they act as if they have done nothing wrong and that they truly are only patriots and heroes. They also are in lock step with one another that they should destroy the current system of government so that they can create a whole brand new model that is based upon dereliction of one's duty to the Constitution itself, and they all seem to be using the Mein Kampf playbook which used emotions and racism and corruption to wrangle in the German public to turn a blind eye to sensible and decent human values and virtues. Number 45 therefore needs to get re-elected in the worse way, so that he can pardon himself and his cronies from all of their pending legal troubles. Because if they are to fundamentally change the Great Experiment into something new and more sinister, then the United States of America, which is the capital of the world, must be turned into this new haven for all of the National Socialist and would be dictators. Now some people have been trying desperately to sound the alarm, that the fascists are coming the fascists are coming, (think Paul Revere of Lynn Massachusetts) but for many reasons which include denial, all of these warnings seem to not being heard or taken seriously.

Now for myself, not being either a democrat or republican has made me see things through a much different lens, and I have always believed in many concepts that both of the two main political parties espouse like: free markets, and more state control, and the concept of individual liberty and justice for all. But I also know criminal and treasonous behavior when I witness it, and all of this at times makes no real sense, because how can you claim to be a patriot when your criminal behavior goes directly against the Constitution and the Framers themselves. **Criminal Behavior.**

Remember that the term **Democracy** itself means a system of government by the whole government or all of the eligible members of a state typically through elected representatives and also is defined as control of a group or organization by the majority of its members. The term **Constitution** itself means a body of fundamental principles or established precedents according to which a state or other organization is acknowledged to be governed.

The **Framers** put all of this into motion, because they were all tired of living under a monarchy representation with a dictatorship twist. So why would we want to go backwards instead of straight-ahead forwards? Thus, in closing why do we need to make America great again for only a few and not the entire whole? When did it ever stop being the great place to live out your dreams in ? Who determined that it had lost its place in the world society? Who determined that because everyone has got a chance to become greater than what they were because of freedom and justice for all was somehow now a bad thing? So thus, in closing I leave you with this:

Booking Photo August 24, 2023

Warning; Don't deny the obvious, know thyself.

Made in the USA
Middletown, DE
28 July 2024